Don Church

The
Holy Bible
in
Rhymed
Verse

The
Holy Bible
in
Rhymed
Verse

Don Church

ISBN: 1-58597-234-7

Library of Congress Control Number: 2003113393

A division of Leathers Publishers, Inc.
4500 College Blvd.
Leawood, KS 66211
1/888/888-7696
www.leatherspublishing.com

Dedicated to

God and His Son Jesus Christ,

who have influenced me

during my life.

CONTENTS

GOD — The Creator 1

ADAM AND EVE — The Cost of Free Advice 3

CAIN AND ABEL — Brotherly Love 5

NOAH — The Ark Builder 6

MRS. NOAH — The Ark Builder's Wife 8

ABRAHAM — Father of the Hebrews 9

LOT — Sodom and Gomorrah 11

ISAAC — Son of Abraham 13

REBEKAH — Number Twos Try Harder 15

JACOB — a.k.a. Israel 16

JOSEPH — The Multicolored Coat 18

MOSES — The Exodus Leader 20

JOSHUA — Jericho and Beyond 22

SAMSON — A Bad Hair Day 24

RUTH — Great-Grandmother of David 26

DAVID — The Rock Star Psalmist 28

SOLOMON — The Wise Man 30

JEREMIAH — Never Too Young 32

ELIJAH — The Greatest Prophet 33

ELISHA — Man of God 35

ESTHER — Savior of Her People 37

JOB — God Did a Job on Job 40

DANIEL — In the Lion's Den 41

JONAH — The Incredible Journey 42

MARY — The Mother of Jesus 44

JOHN THE BAPTIST— The Baptizer 46

JESUS — Son of God 48

THE MAGI — The Wise Women 51

MARY AND MARTHA — A Tale of Two Sisters 52

JUDAS — The Traitor? 53

PETER — The Rock 55

LUKE — The Beloved Physician 57

PAUL — The Great Christian Convert 59

STEPHEN — The Martyr 61

SAINT JOHN — Loyal Apostle 63

SATAN — The Dark Side 64

AND THE REST OF THE STORY 65

INTRODUCTION

There have been a number of translations of the Bible over the years, and although it is the number one book for Christians, very few can recite much about the characters other than a brief description.

I have endeavored to tell about a number of whom I think are the main characters and to add some humor along with their lives, plus tell about them in rhymed verse.

I researched a number of Bibles, but the most of the information was from the Revised Standard Edition, and the grammar follows this.

Since many scholars differ in their translations, many who read this book may not agree with my version of the Bible, but hopefully those who read it will remember my stories and in which I have taken some poetic license.

Some people may think this sacrilegious, but it was not intended to be, and I have been able to reach people with my verses about religious stories without preaching to them.

— *Don Church*

GOD
The Creator

Now, in the beginning
There was only nothing.
God came and said, "Let there be light."
Seeing it was real good,
Separated the dark
From it, and then called the dark "Night."

He then made the Earth
In the midst of the waters,
And Heaven was over the two.
He made vegetation,
Plus plants, seeds and fruit trees;
Then for lights in the sky, He put two.

He created creatures,
The birds and the cattle,
With monsters that swam in the sea.
He ended by adding
A man He called "Adam";
Now, all was as good as could be.

He stopped for the Sabbath,
A day meant for resting;
Then seeing that Adam might grieve
Because he was lonely
Without any helpmate,
He took out a rib and made Eve.

He said they could eat
Anything in the garden,
But of one tree, nary a bite.
Of course, they both did,
So were kicked out of Eden;
He wanted them out of His sight.

All people thereafter
Began with these sinners;
How many is anyone's guess.
So God is now busy
In solving folk's problems —
The world's in a heck of a mess.

He sent down a flood
To wipe out most all people,
To rectify what He had done.
When He tried once more
To give help to the people,
They crucified His only son.

Still God hasn't given
Up on His bad children,
Though often, He has a rough day.
If you are in trouble
And God's help is needed,
To reach Him, you just need to pray.

You might think this isn't
Enough of a story
For all of what God undertook,
But He keeps appearing
In stories of others;
You'll find out when reading this book.

ADAM AND EVE
The Cost of Free Advice

There was Adam and Eve
In this garden one day,
When a serpent came gliding
Up to them to say,
"Can you both eat of all
Of the fruit in this place?"
Eve said, "Well, all but one,"
With a smile on her face.
"But the fruit of one tree,
We're forbidden to try;
As the day that we do,
God has said we will die."

"Oh, now that," said the snake,
"Is a con job for sure.
If you eat of the fruit,
You will always endure,
As one bite of the apple
Will give you new sight.
You will then be like God
And will know wrong from right."

So, when Adam and Eve
Ate the forbidden fruit,
They found out all each wore
Was an old birthday suit.

Can you picture the scene
In this great out-of-doors?
There sat two bloated nudes,
Midst a big pile of cores.

Well, they hastened to make
From some fig leaves, some clothes.
They were plain duds, of course,
Without buttons or bows.

Now the Lord wasn't pleased,
So He gave them some flack;
Plus He said, "Y'all leave,
And don't ever come back.

This, in fact, is the truth
Of what all came to pass,
As the two took advice
From a snake in the grass.

CAIN AND ABEL
Brotherly Love

After Adam and Eve
Were exiled from Eden,
The sons that were born numbered two.
Without any parents
Or sex education,
How did they know just what to do?

Now Cain was a gardener,
Abel a sheepherder.
They sacrificed things to the Lord
Who liked Abel's mutton,
But not Cain's zucchini
And broccoli, which He abhorred.

So Cain killed his brother
Because he was angry;
This was before guns, knives or spears.
When God asked of Cain
What had happened to Abel?
"Am I brother's keeper?" He hears.

So Cain then was banished
From where he was living
And married a woman in Nod.
Since there had been only
Two parents, two brothers,
How this woman happened seems odd.

Since there were no roads then,
It sure wasn't road rage,
Though what he did may seem insane.
But history was made
And folks who act up now
Are said to be out raising Cain.

NOAH
The Ark Builder

God was upset with the people
Whom He scattered all about.
He would rectify the error;
He would simply wipe them out.

But He looked down and saw Noah,
Righteous and religious man.
God decided to take pity
And to modify His plan.

"Get some gopher wood," the Lord said,
"As I plan to save some lives.
Build an ark, a really big one;
Take your spouse, sons and their wives.

"Of all living flesh, go gather
One pair each, female and male."
God told Noah how to build it,
Going over each detail.

After animals were gathered,
Noah buttoned up the doors.
He was lucky that there were no
Elephants or dinosaurs.

Then the rain came down in torrents,
40 days and nights it poured.
Everything outside had perished,
As intended by the Lord.

After seven months, it sat down
On top of Mount Ararat,
But they had to wait five more months
Till the land dried, so they sat.

When they finally departed
From the ark, God blessed them all;
Then He made a covenant
And promised no more big rainfall.

In the sky He put a rainbow,
Though perturbed, if man should sin,
To remind Him of His promise
To not send a flood again.

For three hundred fifty more years,
Noah lived, and when he died,
Noah's sons, Shem, Ham and Japheth,
At God's bidding multiplied.

Their descendants had one language;
They were all of one accord;
Build a tower into Heaven;
This, of course, upset the Lord.

So the Lord confused their language,
Babel was the city's name,
And then scattered them all over —
That's why we don't speak the same.

MRS. NOAH
The Ark Builder's Wife

Everyone has heard how Noah
Built an ark that saved his life,
And the animals he gathered,
But what of poor Noah's wife?

Her home was to be uprooted,
God had told him, Noah said.
She thought building boats on dry land
That he was tetched in the head.

When the water started rising,
And the ark began to float,
All the ladies of her bridge club
Drowned, because they missed the boat.

It was tough to do the cooking
And get clothes dried with the rain,
Plus those in-laws, who were with her,
Just about drove her insane.

After many months of sailing,
She was filled with deep despair,
With no beauty operator
There to do her nails and hair.

When, at last, the journey ended,
Once again, poor Noah's spouse
Was upset, as everybody
Tracked in mud throughout her house.

But the saddest part about it,
Which is really quite a shame,
She was known as "just a housewife,"
And we never learned her name.

ABRAHAM
Father of the Hebrews

He began in life as Abram
And had lived long years in life.
He was sad there were no children
Born by Sarai, his dear wife.

Sarai gave him her slave, Hagar,
For a wife, and things went well.
She conceived and had a son then
That God had named Ishmael.

He said Sarai was his sister
Twice, as be feared for his life,
But each time God intervened
When Pharaohs took her as a wife.

When he was almost 100,
And before a true heir came,
God changed Sarai's name to Sarah;
Abraham was now his name.

Sarah then gave birth to Isaac,
Though both were old at his birth.
God told him that his descendants
Now would populate the Earth.

Sarah got upset with Hagar;
Abraham then forced her out.
But God's angel came to help them;
He possessed a lot of clout.

Abraham was sorely tested,
Told to sacrifice his son.
Just before he lit the fire,
God said it need not be done.

Sarah died, and long years later,
Abraham, a new wife wed.
Started adding to descendants
As God, many times, had said.

His descendants were as many
As God said, and it came true.
But just Ishmael and Isaac,
Long had been the only two.

LOT
Sodom and Gomorrah

Abram's brother was Lot's father;
Therefore when Lot's father died,
Although Abram and wife Sarai
Traveled, Lot was by their side.

As time passed and both men prospered,
They soon came to understand,
They must part, because their cattle
Were too many for the land.

Abram went to live in Canaan;
He was luckier than Lot,
Who went to reside in Sodom;
It was such a wicked spot.

So the Lord dispatched two angels
To tell Lot he had to leave,
As both Sodom and Gomorroh,
Of God's wrath they would receive.

Now, Lot's sons-in-law were skeptics;
Both decided they would stay.
Just Lot, his wife and two daughters
Were the ones to go away.

"Don't look back when you are leaving,"
They were told, "And do not halt."
Lot's wife, though, was just too nosy —
Turned into pillar of salt.

Lot said he would go to Zoar,
But because he wasn't brave,
He, instead, took his two daughters
And they dwelt inside a cave.

With no men to wed, the daughters
Dealt their father quite a blow.
Got him drunk and then they slept with him
For two nights in a row.

Though in Sodom, Lot was righteous,
Had engaged now in incest.
Had God known that this would happen,
Might have killed them with the rest.

ISAAC
Son of Abraham

Now, in the Book of Abraham,
It tells how Isaac's life began.
When it was time for him to wed,
His father came up with a plan.

A servant was dispatched to go
To Nahor with some gifts and gold,
And when a maiden at the well
Would be the right one to behold.

She took him to her father's house;
The servant told why he'd been sent.
Her father said, "It's up to her."
Rebekah said, "I will," and went.

Rebekah soon was Isaac's wife;
When she conceived, events occur.
What happened won't be covered here,
As it is in the book on her.

A famine came upon the land;
The Lord told Isaac not to go
To Egypt, but another place
Because the Lord had told him so.

Now Isaac, just like Abraham,
Who was so fearful for his life,
Informed the King, Rebekah was
His sister, instead of his wife.

The king then took Rebekah in,
But when he found it wasn't true,
He warned people not to touch her
Or it would be their Waterloo.

Now, Isaac stayed there for awhile
And with the Lord's help prospered so
The Philistines filled up the wells.
The king informed him he must go.

Two Hittite wives which Esau had
Gave Isaac and Rebekah fits.
Rebekah told Isaac that she
Was ready to tear them to bits.

Important as Isaac appeared,
And to the Lord was so endeared,
His life should have ended real big —
It seems, though, he just disappeared.

REBEKAH
Number Twos Try Harder

When Rebekah was expecting,
There were times she wished to scream;
So she took her case to God,
Who gave her answers in a dream.

She would have not one, but two kids;
One would be a burly son,
While the other, though less macho,
Would still rule the older one.

Isaac showered love on Esau,
As he was his first-born boy,
While the second, seconds later,
Was his mother's pride and joy.

Jacob was a little tricky;
He did something that was bad,
As he bought his brother's birthright
With a pot of stew he had.

Now, Rebekah said to Jacob,
"You've the birthright, that is true,
But to really be head honcho,
You must get his blessing, too."

Jacob fooled his poor old pappy,
Who was blind, so could not tell
It was he, instead of Esau;
He conned Isaac with the smell.

Since Rebekah's dream convinced her
Who would rule with Isaac gone,
Helped out Jacob, as she knew
Which side her bread was buttered on.

JACOB
a.k.a Israel

Jacob was the son of Isaac
And the younger Esau's twin.
Since Esau would get the blessing,
Jacob found a way to win.

He first bought his brother's birthright
With a bowl of steaming stew;
Then he conned his poor old pappy
And received his blessing, too.

This upset his brother Esau,
So to save his life he fled,
As he feared his macho brother
Might intend to have him dead.

On the way he saw a ladder
From the Heaven to the ground.
In a dream the Lord informed him
That protection was around.

Laban had a daughter, Rachel;
Jacob fell in love with her.
He must work for seven years
Before a wedding could occur.

But his uncle pulled a fast one;
Jacob, next day, found instead
Of beloved Rachel, it was
Sister, Leah, he had wed.

"If you'll serve me seven more years,"
Laban said, "Here's what I'll do,

Spend a week here first with Leah,
Then I'll give you Rachel, too."

Although married to two women,
Jacob loved his Rachel more,
But while Rachel had no children.
Leah's now soon numbered four.

Rachel finally conceived,
And after all was said and done,
With two wives, two maids and 12 sons,
Rachel, though, was number one.

After seven more years, Jacob
Asked to leave though had to stay,
But took family and livestock
And, in secret, went away.

Jacob started back to Canaan,
But met Esau as he neared.
He was welcomed by his brother —
It was not the way he'd feared.

He asked to delay his entry,
Stayed behind and as night fell,
God appeared and these two wrestled —
God said, "You're now Israel."

Jacob ended up in Canaan,
But before his life was done,
Went to Egypt due to Joseph,
His and Rachel's first-born son.

When he died, he told his offspring
Just what each of them would do,
Then was buried back in Canaan
When his life, at last, was through.

JOSEPH
The Multicolored Coat

Though Joseph had 11 brothers,
He was favored more by his dad,
Who gave him a multicolored coat,
An act that made his brothers mad.

He had dreams where all his brothers
Would all bow down to their disdain;
Their jealousy turned into hatred
And plotted to have Joseph slain.

One day they were out in the pasture;
Joseph came, they considered a bit.
They would take his coat but not kill him,
Instead throw him into a pit.

Some Ishmaelites happened by then,
Their plan for him now was rethought.
They offered to sell Joseph to them;
The Ishmaelites promptly bought.

Now Potiphar, Pharaoh's guard captain,
Purchased Joseph, who shortly became
The captain's household overseer
And garnered a small bit of fame.

But Potiphar's wife fell for Joseph;
She pursued him to no avail,
Then claimed Joseph had tried to bed her,
So Joseph was thrown into jail.

He was placed in charge of the prisoners,
Interpreted some of their dreams.

He later was called on by Pharaoh
To interpret his, so it seems.

For seven years would be great harvests;
Then seven years there would be drought.
They should store up grain the first seven,
For when the bad years came about.

The Pharaoh made Joseph head honcho,
And his storage plan worked so well,
When shortages hit other countries,
There was plenty of grain to sell.

Then Joseph's half-brothers came calling,
To Egypt to buy grain, they said;
Did not recognize their own brother,
Whom they, long ago, wanted dead.

He sent them, with grain, back to Canaan,
But Simeon, held hostage, stayed,
Till Benjamin would return with them,
And finally Jacob obeyed.

When Joseph informed them who he was,
What they had done he would forgive.
He told what occurred to the Pharaoh,
Who said they should come there to live.

And so the whole kit and caboodle
Of Joseph's clan came to live there,
Were given the best land in Egypt,
An act, which to most, seems unfair.

It's said truth is stranger than fiction,
So good turned out what had been bad;
To think this may never have happened,
If not for the coat Joseph had.

MOSES
The Exodus

In Egypt, of Israelites' population,
The Pharaoh, it seemed, wasn't thrilled.
In order to keep it from growing much larger,
He ordered their boy babies killed.

Till Moses was three months, was hid by his parents,
Then left by the side of the Nile.
The daughter of Pharaoh discovered and raised him,
Though Israelite, lived in style.

One day Moses killed an Egyptian for beating
A Hebrew, but when he was dead,
Discovered that someone had witnessed the killing,
So, to save his life, Moses fled.

He moved into Midian, lived there with Jethro
And took Jethro's daughter as wife.
He lived 40 years as a quiet sheepherder,
Till a burning bush changed his life.

Long years had passed by since the day he left Egypt,
A new Pharaoh was on the throne.
The Israelites now were under a burden,
And God could hear His children moan.

God wanted His children to exit from Egypt,
And Moses was picked for the task.
A murderer, slow-speaking, lowly sheepherder;
"Why would He pick him?" you might ask.

God sent Brother Aaron to help do the talking;
He turned out to be a poor choice.
But when they left Egypt, the Red Sea was parted;
It seemed like a time to rejoice.

Now, after a long time of roaming the country,
With manna to eat every day,
The people complained that this wasn't an Eden
Where deer and the antelope play.

While Moses was getting the famed 10 commandments,
Left Aaron in charge of the staff.
He conned people into donating their jewelry
And molded a big golden calf.

This upset the Lord who got angry with Moses
And caused them to wander some more.
Because of the idol, plus how the folks acted
While Aaron was minding the store.

After more years of wandering, Aaron succumbed,
Which wasn't a really great loss.
Though this now left Moses to go it alone;
No big deal — he had always been boss.

"I'll show you the Promised Land," Moses was told.
"But you cannot go there," said the Lord."
Moses died and was buried in Moab, not Canaan,
With Heaven his only reward.

JOSHUA
Jericho and Beyond

When Moses was buried,
The mantle was passed on
To Joshua, the son of Nun.
The Lord said, "I'll give you
The land promised Moses;
Now you have to get the job done.

Cross over the Jordan,
Then wait till I tell you,
As I will give you Jericho.
Pick out seven priests who
Will go with their trumpets,
And each time they circle, will blow.

For six days they go once;
The seventh day, seven,
And people will shout as they pass.
The walls will then tumble,
Just like opera singers
Whose high note will shatter fine glass."

Now, when the walls fell,
They killed all of the people
And then burned the town to the ground.
He kept on repeating
This killing and burning,
Till taking the land all around.

This book in the Bible,
With all of the killing,
Which Joshua led all about,
Would make both Genghis Khan
And Attila the Hun
Look a lot less fierce than a Boy Scout.

The land was divided
Among all the people
With lots which old Joshua cast.
Long years had elapsed
Since they crossed over Jordan;
The need for his leading had passed.

And then Joshua died
Just as Moses had done;
His age was one hundred and ten.
Having followed the Lord,
He had claimed all the land;
And then came his final amen.

SAMSON
A Bad Hair Day

There was once a man named Samson
To whom God had given strength.
He was told to never cut his hair,
No matter what the length.

Now, the Philistines were warriors
Samson thought he had to fight.
He possessed such super power
That he killed them left and right.

But he met a girl, Delilah,
Who found out why he was strong.
He said his strength came from hair
Instead of God, and this was wrong.

So, they shaved his head, and bingo,
God departed from the scene.
Mighty Samson was made helpless
By a female Philistine.

Then they blinded and enslaved him,
Had him grinding in the mill.
Though they mocked and made sport of him,
They did not break Samson's will.

As time passed, his hair again grew,
And his strength, it seems, returned.
If his enemies took notice,
They did not appear concerned.

He was taken from the prison;
He was jeered and made to stand
In between two massive pillars —
Samson touched them with each hand.

Then he asked the Lord to give him
Back his strength with his last breath.
When he pushed, he brought the house down,
Thus avenging his own death.

If you're asked from whence your strength come,
Tell them it comes from the Lord.
In this world there are Delilahs,
Who, if met, should be ignored.

RUTH
Great-Grandmother of David

Naomi, her husband
And two sons left Judah;
They went to Moab to save lives.
Then Naomi's husband
Died, and their two sons both
Took women in Moab for wives.

About ten years later,
The sons also perished.
Naomi and daughter-in-laws
Began to leave Moab
And go back to Judah,
As staying there seemed a lost cause.

Naomi told both girls
To go back to Moab.
Orpah went, but Ruth answered, "No."
She just wouldn't listen
To Naomi's pleadings
And said, "Where you go, I will go."

"Where you lodge, I will lodge,
And your people, your God,
Are my people and my God, too.
Where you die, I will die.
May the Lord grant my wish
That I will be buried by you."

Naomi told Ruth
That a close kinsman, Boaz,
Had fields she should go in and glean.
She did this many days,
And the grain which she got,
She would sell on the days in between.

Then Naomi told Ruth,
When Boaz went to sleep,
To lie down at the foot of his bed.
Then when Boaz awoke
And saw Ruth lying there,
Might suggest she lie elsewhere instead.

Now, Naomi had land
She was willing to sell.
The buyer, though, must understand,
As part of the deal,
He would have to wed Ruth,
As she went along with the land.

To shorten the story,
Ruth and Boaz married.
Their first child was a most famous one,
As he fathered Jesse,
And Jesse in turn
Fathered David, or Ruth's great-grandson.

DAVID
The Rock Star Psalmist

When David was a little boy,
His country was at war.
Now neither side was winning,
But there was much blood and gore.

To minimize the slaughtering,
A plan was soon contrived
That when the battle ended,
All but one would have survived.

A giant named Goliath said,
At least, so all recall,
"Let us fight one on one —
Whoever wins will take it all."

As no one else would volunteer,
Young David went alone,
Armed only with a sling shot
And a few small polished stones.

Goliath was insulted,
And, in fact, he roared with rage.
To think that Israel had sent
One of such tender age.

His future was influenced
By the deed he did that morn.
When David killed Goliath,
Then the first "Rock Star" was born.

Because the people praised him,
He was hated by King Saul.
(This wasn't the same Saul
Who later changed his name to Paul.)

As years went by, Saul died, of course,
And David was made king.
So many were his victories,
That praises folks would sing.

Who hasn't heard of David
And of his outstanding life?
Who had Bathsheba's husband killed,
Then took her for his wife.

He was the guy who wrote the Psalms,
A master of the word.
Though he wrote many, still
The greatest was the twenty-third.

But he's remembered mainly
For Goliath's death that day,
And "The Lord Is My Shepherd"
Is the psalm we often say.

SOLOMON
Son of David

Son of David and Bathsheba
Was made King when David died.
Though he had an older brother,
David picked him to preside.

Under his reign, which was brilliant,
Came the zenith of the land;
Was on friendly terms with Egypt
And took Pharaoh's daughter's hand.

In a dream the Lord inquired
What he wished to have consigned.
Solomon asked not for riches,
But an understanding mind.

As this pleased the Lord so greatly,
He said, "I will give to you
More than just the greatest wisdom,
Also wealth and honor, too."

Now the greatest of achievements,
And he had more than a few,
Were rebuilding of the Temple,
Plus a house for the Lord, too.

Then he built himself a palace,
Plus a palace for his spouse.
When the second one was finished,
She went to live in her house.

He received the Queen of Sheba,
Who had heard he was so wise.
After questioning, his wisdom
Was much more, to her surprise.

Now, to build so many structures
Took a lot of slaves and gold;
So life wasn't all that rosy
For those working, it is told.

Now, the King loved foreign women,
And he took some as his wives.
One so wise should have known better —
Trouble, in such case, arrives.

Since the foreign wives had idols,
They soon turned his heart away
From the Lord, toward their idols.
For this, there was hell to pay.

Why would anyone with wisdom
Such as he who knew the score,
And was wed to one good woman,
Care to have a hundred more?

Solomon was then deserted
By the Lord, in anger, who
Said, "I'll tear your kingdom from you,
But not till your life is through."

Solomon, from life, departed;
He had such a glowing start,
Though considered once the wisest,
At the end, was not too smart.

JEREMIAH
Never Too Young

God told Jeremiah, "Before you were born,
You were consecrated and picked for a task.
"But, God," Jeremiah said, "I am a youth,
So I am unable to do what you ask."

God said, "There are nations and kingdoms to rule;
Don't say you're too young, just go do as I say."
Therefore Jeremiah went as God commanded,
But with reservations and filled with dismay.

However, he did what God told him to do,
Gave up the belief he was really too young.
He rose to the task and his great deeds were many;
So there in the Bible his praises are sung.

Just like Jeremiah, we too may be called
By God to accomplish what He may request.
We hope when it comes we will not make excuses,
But will have the courage to go do our best.

ELIJAH
The Greatest Prophet

Now, Elijah was a prophet
Who was favored by the Lord.
He was sent to talk to Ahab
And was not to be ignored.

Jezebel, the wife of Ahab,
Was an idolatry sort,
Wanted Baal and not Jehovah
The religion of the court.

He told Ahab, that for three years,
That the land would have a drought.
He left and was fed by ravens —
Not one which Poe wrote about.

When the brook he drank from dried up,
The Lord came with an appeal.
Go to Zarephart, where a widow
Will serve you bread made from meal.

Though the meal was just a handful,
Bread was constantly supplied,
But the widow was in anguish
When her son who lived there died.

So Elijah took him upstairs
And three times implored the Lord
To have mercy on this poor child,
So the son's life was restored.

Back to Ahab went Elijah;
He was sent there to foretell

People there should choose Jehovah,
Whereas they now worshipped Baal.

Two bulls picked for sacrificing
Would be placed on unlit wood.
Baal prophets would call to heaven
To bring fire if they could.

Hours passed, but their beseeching
Didn't bring down Baal to rule.
Then Elijah mocked them saying
Baal was just a bunch of bull.

So another bull was taken,
Cut up, placed just as before.
Then the wood was soaked with water —
Fire came down with a roar.

This convinced them of the true God;
All Baal prophets were then slain.
Ahab was told go and drink now —
Heard the sound of falling rain.

Now, to make the story shorter,
What occurred next, we will skip,
And fast forward to Elijah
Leaving on a final trip.

Going with him was Elisha,
Who stuck with him every day;
Asked Elijah for his spirit
On the day he went away.

Then a chariot of fire,
Drawn by fire horses, too,
Took Elijah into Heaven—
This great prophet's life was through.

ELISHA
Man of God

When Elijah went to heaven,
Friend Elisha watched his ride.
He picked up Elijah's mantel,
Crossed to Jordan's other side.

Now Elisha was a prophet.
When he was at Jericho,
He was told of the bad water;
Nothing in the land would grow.

He threw salt into the water;
It was wholesome right away.
He said that the Lord had blessed it;
It's still wholesome to this day.

The king of Israel once asked
For help against the Moabites.
The Lord was called upon for help;
Wars were won by the Israelites.

He raised a little boy from death;
He cleansed a man with leprosy.
He restored vision to the blind
And led a king to victory.

Elisha got upset at times.
"Get your own prophets," he began,
But they thought him a man of God,
So they insisted, "You the man."

The king of Syria was ill.
"You will get well," Elisha said.
The servant told, he'd now be king,
Smothered the king till he was dead.

No man can live forever, even
Though the Lord is by his side.
Elisha then slept with his fathers,
Which, in those days, meant he died.

ESTHER
Savior of Her People

King Ahasuerus called his Queen
To come — she never came.
The men were quite upset and feared
Their wives would do the same.

They conned him into dumping her
And get a young new queen.
A sort of lovely trophy wife —
If you know what I mean.

They got a lot of virgin girls,
And one the king would choose.
It seemed an honor, plus an offer,
No girl could refuse.

Now Esther was a captive
Brought from Judah years before,
And people didn't know that
She was Jewish any more.

Her mother and her father both
Died as the years went by;
Now was adopted daughter
Of her cousin, Mordecai.

He helped Esther get selected
As one of the chosen few,
But he cautioned her to never
Tell a soul she was a Jew.

And after many months, of course,
The outcome could be seen,
Because the King loved Esther most,
He chose her for his Queen.

Two eunuchs who were guards at gates
Planned to do in the King,
But Mordecai found out and sent
A warning through the Queen.

The two were promptly hanged, and Haman
Was made the Head Prince.
Then all bowed down but Mordecai,
Who would not give an inch.

This bothered Haman very much,
And he was so annoyed,
He had the King sign orders
To have all the Jews destroyed.

The King learned that the one
Who saved his life was surely due
A big reward — made Mordecai
Head Honcho Number Two.

When Esther told the King about
The gallows Haman built,
The King decided Haman should
Be punished for his guilt.

So Haman was hanged on the gallows
50 cubits high.
The one he built to hang the one
He hated — Mordecai.

When Esther told the King what orders
He had signed would do,
Would have her people killed
As they were just like her, a Jew.

The King, of course, retracted them,
As Esther was so brave,
And due to his great love for her,
Her people's lives were saved.

JOB
God Did a Job on Job

In ancient days, a man named Job
Was great, extremely rich, and yet
He had 10 kids and loved the Lord;
His life was ruined by a bet.

When God said, "See my servant, Job,
An honest and an upright man?"
When Satan said, "You guard him so,"
God said, "Go change him, if you can."

So Satan had Job's wealth removed;
Then had his sons and daughters killed.
But Job did neither curse his God
Nor lose the faith God had instilled.

So Satan had another chance
And gave Job sores from foot to head.
Still, Job did not lose faith in God,
Although he wished that he were dead.

Job was deserted by his friends,
All who accused him of great sin.
Yet, though he didn't understand
What happened, Job did not give in.

Job's lamentations lasted long,
But just to make the story short,
His wealth and family were restored,
And he was great at last report.

We hope we never have Job's fate,
Yet, if misfortune comes our way,
We trust we will not lose our faith,
But stay the course like Job, we pray.

DANIEL
In the Lions' Den

You've all read of Daniel,
How he could interpret
The dreams of the rulers and kings.
However, their wizards
Would all be dumbfounded,
But Daniel told them many things.

Since Daniel was honored,
The flunkies, in anger,
Suggested a law the king bought —
That anyone breaking
Be fed to the lions,
And Daniel, by praying, was caught.

When Daniel was tossed in
The den with the lions,
It seemed he would meet with defeat,
But God made the lions
Think Daniel was broccoli,
And lions, of course, just eat meat.

However, the people
Who caused all these problems
Discovered just how the blood runs.
The lions were looking
At juicy hamburgers,
So ate them without any buns.

Now most of the people,
On reading this story,
May think that it sounds a bit odd.
The truth that is hidden
In this Bible passage —
It doesn't pay to mess with God.

JONAH
The Incredible Journey

Since those who lived in Nineveh
Were wicked, "Jonah," said the Lord,
"Go read the riot act to them."
He found a ship and got aboard.

Now Jonah thought, "Those men are mean,
I, probably, could end up dead."
He didn't go to Nineveh,
But sailed the other way instead.

Since Jonah disobeyed the Lord,
He had him tossed into the sea,
Where he was swallowed by a whale.
It was so dark he could not see.

He didn't have a thing to read;
He didn't like what was inside,
And since the whale swam up and down,
He got real seasick from the ride.

There were times he was short of air,
And what there was had quite a smell.
He couldn't get the evening news;
Also, he couldn't sleep too well.

Each time the whale would take in food,
Like plankton, small fish or a plant,
Poor Jonah would get soaking wet,
Which was a constant irritant.

So Jonah pleaded loud and long
And promised he would sin no more.
The Lord gave in and told the whale
To throw up Jonah on the shore.

The whale was happy to oblige;
Three days his stomach was upset.
Now, Jonah ever afterwards,
Would never touch fish on a bet.

Presented is this sage advice:
If you do not accept God's views,
Like Jonah, He may give to you
An offer you cannot refuse.

MARY
The Mother of Jesus

Mary was young and unmarried;
She was puzzled and yet awed
When an angel told her she would have
A son fathered by God.

Joseph, her intended husband,
Was upset when he found out
She was pregnant, and her story
Left him filled, somewhat, with doubt.

Now he didn't want to shame her,
So the wedding would go on,
But he'd quietly divorce her;
In a short time, she'd be gone.

Gabriel then came to Joseph;
After hearing what he said,
Joseph changed his mind completely.
Shortly afterward they wed.

A decree came out from Caesar,
Everyone should be enrolled.
Mary and her husband Joseph
Went to Bethlehem as told.

Their room was a lowly manger;
She gave birth that very night.
What with angels, star and shepherds,
It was really quite a sight.

After giving birth to Jesus,
God warned Joseph in a dream
To rise up and flee to Egypt,
To escape King Herod's scheme.

Though revered by many people,
And most Christians will concur,
Although she was Jesus' mother,
Not much was written of her.

One day at a wedding, Mary
Told her son, "We're out of wine."
Jesus filled six jars with water;
He turned into wine so fine.

At his crucifixion, Jesus,
Just before his life was done,
He looked down and said to Mary,
"Mother, please behold your son."

JOHN THE BAPTIST
The Baptizer

Elizabeth, in her old age,
Was six months pregnant with a son
When Mary heard from Gabriel,
She was to be the chosen one.

Now Zechariah, too, was told
His wife, old also, would conceive,
And Zechariah was struck mute,
Due to his failure to believe.

So when the baby boy was born,
The silence of his tongue was gone.
All thought he'd be named after Dad,
But he declared his name was "John."

John spent years in the wilderness,
Until God called on him to preach.
He told the people to repent
And baptized all those he could reach.

Some people thought he was the Christ,
But John would not accept their views.
He baptized all with water while
The Holy Spirit, Christ, would use.

When Jesus came from Galilee
To be baptized by John, he found
Though John did so, he thought that it
Should be the other way around.

When Jesus was baptized, he rose;
The heavens opened overhead.
"Thou art my own beloved son
With whom I am well pleased," God said.

Now John reproved Herod the king,
Because his brother's wife he wed.
Herodias was filled with hate
And schemed to see that John was dead.

When Herod's birthday banquet came,
Herodias then saw a chance,
Arranging for her daughter to
Charm Herod with a pleasing dance.

Since Herod liked her dance so much,
"I'll grant you anything," he said.
Solome, at her mother's wish,
Said, "Give me John the Baptist's head."

This saddened Herod very much
Because he feared John was God's friend,
But he could not break oaths he gave,
And so John's life came to an end.

JESUS
God's Only Son

As it had long been prophesied,
The Son of God would come one day
In Bethlehem, of virgin birth,
And it occurred in just that way.

A manger out behind an inn,
Beneath a bright and shining star,
Some shepherds watched and angels sang.
Three wise men journeyed from afar.

He was named Jesus by the Lord.
Soon afterward, he had to flee
To Egypt, since boys under two
Were killed, due Herod's decree.

Now Joseph was told in a dream:
Leave Egypt now that Herod's dead,
To go to Israel to live.
They went to Nazareth instead.

When he was in Jerusalem,
The Elders thought it a surprise
The way he talked and questions asked
By one just 12, but yet so wise.

When he began his ministry,
He gathered mostly fishermen.
He said if they would follow him,
He would make them fishers of men.

Now, John the Baptist baptized him,
And then with the baptism done,
A voice from heaven proudly said,
"I'm pleased with my beloved son."

He preached in temples and outside,
To just a few or multitude.
He took three loaves and seven fish
And turned them into piles of food.

He cleansed some lepers, restored sight;
He raised the dead and healed the sick.
His answered were in parables
To Pharisees who tried to trick.

He saved a prostitute from death
From stoning by some sinning men.
He said a person first must die
In order to be born again.

Though his disciples followed him,
And when he preached, were close at hand.
Watched him performing miracles;
However, did not understand.

He met with both Gentile and Jew.
He walked on water, calmed the sea.
He journeyed to Jerusalem,
Though he knew there his death would be.

He gathered his disciples there,
Ate with them in the Upper Room.
Informed them he would be betrayed
By one of them, told of his doom.

Falsely accused and put in jail,
The jury rigged when he was tried.
Then Pontius Pilate passed the buck;
On Friday, he was crucified.

The tomb was empty Sunday morn,
His body gone, as well as clothes.
He met with some disciples, then
Later that day, Jesus arose.

We pause each year when Easter comes
And wonder how life would have been
If Jesus had not been on earth —
If he had not died for our sin.

———————

So much more could be written
About Jesus, it is true;
However, in the space allowed —
Just this will have to do.

THE MAGI
The Wise Women

If it had been wise women
Who appeared when Christ was born,
They would have brought some diapers
And some blankets that cold morn.

A baby has no use for myrrh
Or frankincense or gold.
They would have brought some hot food
To alleviate the cold.

Would not have been like wise men
Who arrived there 12 days late.
They would have come that morning,
It was such a special date.

They wouldn't have brought bottles,;
Kids were breast fed way back then.
Remember, too, the Bible
Is the works mostly of men.

If it had been that women
Were the wise ones who were there,
There would have been no mention
Of the Magi anywhere.

MARY AND MARTHA
A Tale of Two Sisters

One day, Mary sat and listened
At his feet, as Jesus preached;
While her sister, Martha, labored
And, in anger, she beseeched
Him to make her sister help her;
Jesus, though, did not concur.
He said Mary's chosen portion
Would not be removed from her.

If my wife is busy cooking
While I'm looking at TV,
Should she get upset, I tell her,
That's how Luke says it should be.
In the real world, if we're hungry,
After all is done and said,
We are grateful for the Marthas,
When the time comes to be fed.

JUDAS
The Traitor?

One Disciple was named Judas,
A name linked to infamy.
Maybe what brought him dishonor
Wasn't what it seemed to be.

He's been labeled as a traitor
As his deed was dastardly,
But he had been picked by Jesus
To fulfill a prophecy.

If he had a lust for money,
With the way they ran the shop,
As the treasurer of Jesus,
Could have skimmed some off the top.

Jesus was a well-known person,
So the mystery is this:
Why the need for pointing him out
By his own man with a kiss?

Judas may have thought that Jesus
Would win a big victory
Were he forced to use his powers —
Be the king he ought to be.

If so, he miscalculated,
And the scheme failed that he tried.
Jesus didn't use such powers,
And so he was crucified.

Now, the silver, 30 pieces,
He received for his foul deed
May have only been a smoke screen
Jesus foes mistook for greed.

After Judas saw what happened,
Was distraught to great degree.
Failed in giving back the silver
And hung himself from a tree.

PETER
The Rock

He began in life as Simon,
Was a fisherman by trade.
One day Christ asked him to follow;
Without question, he obeyed.

Jesus soon had 12 disciples,
Then his mission was begun.
All supposedly were equal —
Simon, though, was number one.

Jesus changed his name to Peter,
And he said, "You are my rock,
You will build my church upon it";
It's now shelter for his flock.

Just before Christ's crucifixion,
They met in the Upper Room.
Jesus spoke of blood and body,
And then he told of his doom.

Jesus said, "You will deny me."
Peter cried, "That isn't so,"
But denied him thrice that night
Before the cock began to crow.

After Jesus had ascended,
Peter did as Christ had done,
Healing, traveling and preaching
About Christ, God's only son.

He was persecuted often
By the leaders of the Jews
Who were upset by his preaching
Which was counter to their views.

He wrote letters while in prison
And was finally crucified,
But head down as he requested,
To not die as Christ had died.

LUKE
The Beloved Physician

Luke was known as the physician,
Though we think of him today,
Not for medicine he practiced,
But for what he had to say.

As the author of one gospel
Of Christ's life that's read by all,
And of Acts of the Apostles,
Plus the trips he took with Paul.

Luke did not have Jewish parents —
Was a Christian early on,
Also kept a diary about
The trips on which he'd gone.

Luke had never been with Jesus;
Had not heard him — just the same
Luke wrote quite a lengthy gospel
Giving glory to Christ's name.

He wrote of Saul's great conversion,
And he traveled with him, too.
Plus his medical advice
May have affected Jesus' view.

He was in Rome with Paul also
At the time that Paul was tried.
He apparently departed
Shortly after Paul had died.

Afterwards, he spread the Gospel —
Very few dispute the facts
That he was the author of
The book of Luke, and also Acts.

Of his death, not much is certain.
When and how is left in doubt.
Still, he was quite influential
In the years he was about.

PAUL
The Great Christian Convert

It was in the town of Tarsus
Where the life of Saul began.
He was born of Jewish parents;
He was a religious man.

He was schooled to be a rabbi;
In Jerusalem, he met
Members of the high Sanhedrin
And from them he was to get

Order to pursue the Christians,
Which he did with greatest haste.
He sent many into prison;
Plus he laid the church to waste.

He was there when they stoned Stephen
Who was preaching for the Lord,
But Saul soon would get an offer,
To refuse, could not afford.

As he journeyed to Damascus,
He beheld a brilliant light
Which came down from out the heavens,
And it robbed him of his sight.

Then he heard the voice of Jesus,
"Saul, why persecuteth me?"
Saul became Paul, and a Christian,
And soon after, he could see.

The disciples were suspicious,
Thinking it was very strange,
But he made so many converts,
They were pleased to see the change.

Paul began on his first journey,
Starting churches as he went.
Preaching to both Jew and Gentile,
Spreading his enlightenment.

He wrote letters to the people
Telling what they ought to do,
And because of his crusading,
Numbers of the churches grew.

He went on three lengthy journeys,
Starting churches as he went,
But in synagogues, his preaching
Met with heated great dissent.

After long years was arrested,
Was in prison quite a while,
But he wouldn't let them send him
To Jerusalem for trial.

As a citizen and Roman,
Rome was where he must be tried.
After two years spent in prison,
He was freed and went outside.

During Nero's persecutions,
Many Christians there were killed.
It was thought Paul was beheaded —
This great Christian's life was stilled.

STEPHEN
The Martyr

The apostles were out preaching;
The disciples' numbers grew.
It was plain they needed others,
So their ranks were added to.

They chose seven more good persons;
Stephen was a chosen one,
Full of faith and Holy Spirit,
Many wonders were begun.

Now some synagogues' main members
Disagreed with what he said,
So they stirred up scribes and elders
As they wanted Stephen dead.

They brought him before the Council
With false witnesses to claim
He spoke against this holy place —
Did acts in Jesus' name.

He told of Abraham and how
The 12 tribes got their start.
Claimed they, not he, were breaking laws.
He spoke with all his heart.

They cried out with loud voices
And rushed him and cast him out.
Then stoned to death this Christian
Who was truthful and devout.

And one who watched and gave assent
Was one then known as Saul,
Who later was converted,
And Christ changed his name to Paul.

St. Stephen was a martyr,
The first Christian stoned to death.
He prayed for those stoned him —
Then he took his final breath.

SAINT JOHN
Loyal Apostle

John, the Saint, was an apostle,
Maybe most loyal of all.
He and brother, James the elder,
Early answered Jesus' call.

He accompanied Jesus often;
He was at Gethsemane,
At his trial and crucifixion
Where Christ met his destiny.

Jesus, hanging on the cross, said,
Just before his life was gone,
That the care of Mother Mary
He was leaving up to John.

He preached and he taught with Peter,
But another thing of note
Are the gospel and three letters
Which, supposedly, he wrote.

He lived in a cave in Patmos
With a stone floor for a bed,
And a hole cut in the cave wall
Was a pillow for his head.

There he wrote of revelations
That, from Jesus, he'd received.
It should scare to death all sinners,
If his message is believed.

SATAN
The Dark Side

Some folks don't believe in Satan,
Which is hard to understand,
With the troubles in the Bible,
In which Satan had a hand.

He came disguised as a serpent,
Tempted Eve — she took the bait.
Adam also ate the apple —
That's when God gave them the gate.

Job was sure messed up by Satan,
And the Lord gave his okay.
Every place there were some sinners,
Satan helped lead them astray.

Three times Satan tempted Jesus;
They were on a mountaintop.
Each was met with a refusal;
Satan's sales talk was a flop.

Satan's actions would fill pages,
But a little is enough.
This is just to show ignoring him
Could turn out to be tough.

Satan has a place in Hades,
He will gladly take you in.
In a battle for your soul,
You must pray hard for God to win.

AND THE REST OF THE STORY

Many people in the Bible
Are not included in this book.
This is an invitation, though,
To get a Bible — take a look.

To read of Nehemiah, Joel,
Diana, Micah, Malachi,
Ezekiel, Ezra, Absolom,
Ananias, Maccabees, Haggai.

Plus Caiphas and Gideon,
Ahad, Eli, Bartholomew,
Josiah, Titus, Amos, Mark,
Jude, Lazarus, Nimrod, Matthew.

Hosea, Samuel, Timothy
Were some that didn't make the scene,
Plus Nicodemus, Simeon,
James, Nathan, Mary Magdalene.

There's more that are not listed here,
But read the Bible — you'll concede
Of all the books you'll read that it's
The greatest book you'll ever read.

Other books by Don Church:

- FROM A TREE HOUSE
- The Lord's Prayer
- The Lord Is My Shepherd
- Do You Know What?
- THE COLOR OF HOPE
- The Competitor's Prayer Book
- It Began In Bethlehem
- FROM ANOTHER TREE HOUSE
- ONE BRICK SHORT OF A LOAD